Weird Wo...
WORK
Alison Hawes

Badger Publishing Limited
Oldmedow Road,
Hardwick Industrial Estate,
King's Lynn PE30 4JJ
Telephone: 01438 791037

www.badgerlearning.co.uk

2 4 6 8 10 9 7 5 3 1

The Weird World of Work ISBN 978-1-78464-115-3

Text © Alison Hawes 2015

Complete work © Badger Publishing Limited 2015

All rights reserved. No part of this publication may be reproduced, stored in any form or by any means mechanical, electronic, recording or otherwise without the prior permission of the publisher.

The right of Alison Hawes to be identified as author of this work has been asserted by her in accordance with the Copyright, Designs and Patents Act 1988.

Publisher: Susan Ross
Senior Editor: Danny Pearson
Publishing Assistant: Claire Morgan
Designer: Fiona Grant
Series Consultant: Dee Reid

Photos: Cover Image: © Chuck Nacke/Alamy
Page 5: © shotstock/Alamy
Page 6: Global Warming Images/REX
Page 8: © Amoret Tanner/Alamy
Page 9: © Peter Cavanagh/Alamy
Page 10: © Pictorial Press Ltd/Alamy
Page 11: © Universal Images Group Limited/Alamy
Page 12: LUIGI NOCENTI/REX
Page 13: FLPA/REX
Page 14: Qilai Shen/REX
Page 15: The Independent/REX
Page 16: REX
Page 17: Design Pics Inc/REX
Page 18: © The Keasbury-Gordon Photograph Archive/Alamy
Page 20: ITV/REX
Page 21: Roger-Viollet/REX
Page 22: Geoffrey Robinson/REX
Page 24: © Visions of America, LLC/Alamy
Page 25: © christopher Pillitz/Alamy
Page 26: Sipa Press/REX
Page 27: Joe Pepler/REX
Page 28: Sipa Press/REX
Page 29: © JH Kuva/Alamy
Page 30: Unimedia Images/REX

Attempts to contact all copyright holders have been made.
If any omitted would care to contact Badger Learning, we will be happy to make appropriate arrangements.

Weird World of WORK

Contents

1. Dirty and disgusting — 5
2. More dirty and disgusting jobs — 11
3. Dangerous jobs — 17
4. The most dangerous jobs — 22
5. Four unusual jobs — 27

Questions — 31

Index — 32

Vocabulary

chemicals		forensic
confiscated		hazardous
entomologist	phosphorous
environments	poisonous

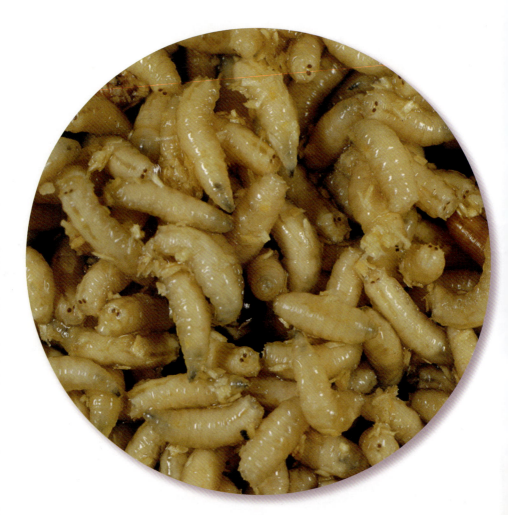

1. Dirty and disgusting

Would you like to do a job where you have to get your hands dirty, like scraping the fat off animal skins or being a sewage worker?

Long ago people did many jobs that were dirty or disgusting, or both! Some of these jobs were dirty because people had to handle a lot of mud, muck and poo!

Nobody wanted to do these jobs but sometimes they were the only jobs they could get.

Gong farmer

More than 700 years ago, many people emptied their sewage into the street or river. But some towns had toilets that emptied into a big pit.

There may have been only 16 toilets for 30,000 people! When these pits were full, it was the gong farmer's job to empty them. This was a very smelly job.

Gong farmers worked at night, so no-one would see them (or smell them!) at work.

The dung was collected in big barrels and taken outside the town or city where it was used as fertiliser for market gardens and farms.

Tools: Shovel, buckets and barrels
Dirt: Human poo
Danger: Poisonous fumes from the cesspits
Pay: About sixpence a day
(That's about 2½p)

Street orderly

In Victorian times, horses were the only means of transport.

All those horses meant lots of horse poo and it was the street orderly's job to remove it. He had to sweep away the dung to the side of the road.

Tools: Brush and shovel
Dirt: Horse poo and mud
Danger: Dodging the traffic and horses' hooves
Pay: About six shillings a week (That's about 30p!)

Many street orderlies were young boys who worked for very long hours.

If the horse dung was not swept away quickly it would be squashed down into the mud of the road and then the boys would have to get a scraper and scrape off the poo.

WOW! facts

In Victorian times, 100 tons of horse poo was removed from the streets of London every day!

Mudlark

In Victorian London, many children worked as mudlarks in the River Thames.

When the tide was out, they would spend hours poking around in the stinking mud for anything they could sell, such as coal, fat, metal or wood.

Unfortunately, the police often confiscated the items they found.

> **Tools:** Bag
> **Dirt:** Human poo, dead animals, factory pollution
> **Danger:** From drowning, disease and the police
> **Pay:** A few pence a day

2. More dirty and disgusting jobs

Armpit sniffer

Nowadays, machines are often used to do a lot of the dirty or disgusting jobs that most of us wouldn't want to do by hand. However, there are still some gross jobs that machines can't do.

Before deodorants are put on sale, they first have to be tested to make sure they work.

This means someone has to spend their day sniffing other people's armpits. Nice!

Forensic entomologist

A forensic entomologist studies dead bodies and the insects living on the bodies, when they are found.

The entomologist can often help the police solve crimes, such as murder.

A forensic entomologist has to dig out maggots from the body to work out when the person died. Or they may look at the insect poo to work out if the person had been drugged.

Maggot farmer

A maggot farmer produces tons of live maggots.

The farmer keeps billions of flies in the fly room. The flies lay their eggs on trays of raw meat. When the eggs hatch into maggots, the farmer feeds them on more raw meat to fatten them up for sale.

WOW! facts

The worst part of being a maggot farmer is the smell. Hungry maggots stink of wee!

HAZMAT diver

Being a HAZMAT diver is one of the dirtiest and most dangerous jobs in the world!

This is because HAZMAT divers spend most of their day next to toxic chemicals and waste.

HAZMAT is short for **haz**ardous **mat**erials.

Jobs a HAZMAT diver does:
- unclogs sewer pipes
- fixes leaks in oil pipes
- cleans up after chemical spills
- finds dead bodies

Just one small tear in a diver's suit could lead to the diver becoming very ill or being badly injured. So, HAZMAT divers wear a specially designed diving suit that has gloves and boots attached, so no toxic materials can get through to the diver's skin.

A HAZMAT diver's suit is cleaned of all toxic materials before it is removed.

3. Dangerous jobs

Today, there are lots of rules to prevent people getting hurt or ill at work.

Many workers have to wear special safety equipment to keep them safe from dangerous situations and toxic materials.

Long ago, however, there were very few safety rules. It may surprise you to know that some of the most dangerous work was carried out by children.

Match girl

In Victorian times, many girls and young women made matches for a living.

The work was boring and very poorly paid. Also the girls had money taken from their wages if they:
- were late
- talked
- dropped matches
- went to the toilet

But the worst thing about being a match girl was that it was so dangerous.

Matches were made by dipping small wooden sticks into a toxic chemical called white phosphorous.

The poisonous fumes from the phosphorous meant many girls developed a horrid disease called phossy jaw.

Symptoms of phossy jaw:
- toothache
- swollen gums
- infected jawbone
- intense pain
- a foul-smelling pus from the jawbone

The only cure was to remove the jawbone.

Scavenger

Scavengers worked in the Victorian cotton mills. They had to crawl under the machines to pick up the bits of cotton that fell onto the floor.

The space under the machines was about 80 centimetres, so this job could only be done by small children.

Children worked from 5.30am to 8pm each day. Many children accidently got their fingers or arms chopped off. Some children were crushed by the machines.

Climbing boy

In Victorian times, climbing boys worked for chimney sweeps. Their job was to climb up the narrow chimneys and brush the soot away. It was a dangerous and filthy job.

Some of the dangers were:
- becoming stuck in a chimney
- being suffocated by soot
- being injured or killed in a fall
- being burned
- skin cancer

WOW! facts

Climbing boys were not paid! They worked for their food and a place to sleep.

4. The most dangerous jobs

Even though today, there are lots of health and safety rules at work, some jobs are more dangerous than others.

Which jobs do you think are really dangerous? Working as a firefighter or as a stunt performer?

Guess what? Being a builder is far more dangerous than both of those jobs!

Here are some of the most dangerous jobs in the world:

The job	The dangers
Mechanic	Sharp tools, heavy machinery, toxic fumes
Builder/ construction worker	Sharp tools, heavy materials, toxic fumes, heights
Search and rescue	Extreme weather, freezing temperatures, difficult terrain
Sanitation worker	Hazardous and toxic waste
Land mine remover	Explosives
Rickshaw, tuk tuk taxi driver	Traffic accidents, poor road conditions, robbery, violence
Miner	Roof falls, flooding, toxic gas, health problems

The top three most dangerous jobs

Number three - bush pilot

Being a bush pilot is the third most dangerous job in the world!

Bush pilots fly small aircraft into some of the most remote places on Earth, such as the icy lands of Alaska or the dense bush of Africa.

They have to deal with:
- severe weather
- weather that changes very quickly
- landing on bumpy ground

If they make one tiny mistake it can lead to disaster!

Number two - deep sea fisherman

Deep sea fishermen do the second most dangerous job in the world. They spend days or weeks at sea, in some of the most hostile environments on earth.

To catch the fish we eat, they often have to deal with:
- freezing temperatures
- rough weather
- sudden storms
- icy decks
- heavy machinery

Every year, many deep sea fishermen are badly injured or die at work.

Number one - lumberjack

The number one most dangerous job in the world is logging, which is what lumberjacks do.

A lumberjack can never be 100% sure where the tree they are cutting is going to fall!

Lumberjacks use big chainsaws and heavy machinery to cut, lift and transport the logs. There is always danger from high winds and falling trees and branches.

WOW! facts
In 2012, 62 loggers were killed just in America.

5. Four unusual jobs

If you don't fancy working in a factory or an office and you want to do something that's different from everybody else, then one of these jobs might be just what you're looking for.

Snake milker

A snake milker catches poisonous snakes and extracts their venom. The venom is used to make anti-venom to treat people bitten by deadly snakes.

But snake milkers have to be careful not to get bitten themselves!

Sports mascot

Most professional sports teams have a mascot. If you are an energetic, fun person, this might be just the job for you.

Mascots entertain fans at games and appear at events to promote their sports club. They do all of this without speaking!

Sports mascots mustn't mind making a fool of themselves!

Dog food taster

Yes, this job really does exist! It may sound rather gross but pet food companies employ food scientists to smell, taste and judge the cat and dog food they sell.

The food taster checks for flavours and textures they know cats and dogs will like.

Although pet food tasters chew the food, they do not swallow it!

Lego builder

Would you like to be paid to play with Lego all day?

Lego builders create and repair Lego models at the Legoland theme parks and Lego discovery centres across the world.

There are only 40 Lego master builders in the world, so it might not be the easiest job to get!

WOW! facts

There are about 80 Lego bricks in the world for every person on Earth!

Questions

What did a mudlark do? *(page 10)*

What is the most disgusting part of maggot farming? *(page 13)*

Why did scavengers have to be children? *(page 20)*

What dangers do miners face at work? *(page 23)*

What is the most dangerous job in the world and why? *(page 26)*

What type of person would make a good sports mascot? *(page 28)*

Index

animal skins 5
barrels 7
builder 22, 30
cesspits 7
chainsaws 26
chemical 15, 19
climbing boys 21
confiscated 10
cotton mills 20
deep sea fishermen 25
dog food 29
deodorants 11
dung 7-8
fertiliser 7
forensic entomologist 12
fumes 7, 19, 23
gong farmer 6
HAZMAT diver 14-15, 16
maggot 13, 31
mudlarks 10
police 10,12
rickshaw 23
sanitation 23
sewer 15
snake milker 27
toxic 14, 16-17, 19, 23
venom 27
white phosphorous 19